Fashion Design Illustration

Men

Patrick John Ireland

B T Batsford Ltd, London

Printed in the UK by The Bath Press
for the publishers
B. T. Batsford Ltd
4 Fitzhardinge Street
London W1H 0AH

ISBN 0 7134 6623 5

A CIP catalogue record for this book is available from the British Library.

Acknowledgements

Images on pp32, 35, 37, 56, 59, 60, 62 courtesy of the
Next Directory.

Photograph on p2 by Rainer Usselmann.

I would like to extend my thanks to the Bournemouth College of Art and Design,
Berkshire College of Art, the Cordwainer's College, London and all the students and
lecturers in the many colleges and workshops I have worked with for their encourage-
ment in producing this book.

Thanks also to Richard Reynolds and Martina Stansbie, my editors at BT Batsford Ltd.

Fashion Design Illustration

Men

Contents

Introduction

The purpose of this book is to introduce fashion drawing techniques. It will help students who are considering undertaking a design course, students in the early stages of such a course, and those studying part-time. It shows how to develop drawing skills from simple, basic methods to more advanced techniques, ranging from figure drawing to design sketching, working drawings and presentation techniques, and will give students the confidence to communicate their design ideas on paper.

The designer should possess a general awareness of fashion, and a sound knowledge of fabrics and the use of colour. He or she should be capable of finding inspiration from many different sources and should be able to develop these ideas to create original designs. Some knowledge of pattern-cutting and the methods of making up garments are also necessary requirements.

This book is arranged in sections to cover the different stages in the fashion process. It shows how to develop the fashion figure, working from the basic body proportions, by creating and utilizing figure templates. In the early stages, the designer can copy or trace templates directly from this book and develop design ideas over them with the aid of semi-transparent paper or a light box.

A fashion designer needs to develop a style of drawing which is clear, fluent and adaptable. Costume and life classes are extremely helpful and should be attended if at all possible. The different methods illustrated in this book should help the student to produce both attractive and functional fashion design drawings.

There are three stages of drawing when designing:

1 Design development
In the early stages of developing a design, sketches should be fairly rough, exploring and experimenting with the many possibilities within each idea or theme. At this point, these groups of drawings are known as design development sheets. They should indicate design ideas and illustrate both the front and the back of the garments. The type of material and its pattern and texture should also be suggested, perhaps with a sample fabric attached to the sheet. Notes can be added to convey any details not shown on the sketch.

2 Production drawings
When a design has been approved, a sample garment will be requested. The production team will need a specification sheet and a production drawing of the design for this purpose. This drawing has to be clear and diagrammatic in order to show details of the cut, seam and dart placement as well as any proposed style features.

3 Presentation drawings
Presentation drawings are used to present a collection of design ideas to a client. They should be finished drawings which project the intended fashion image of the designs. This means that careful thought should be given not only to the drawing of the garments but also to the overall effect, including the pose of the figures, hairstyles and accessories. Different ways of presenting the work should also be developed, taking into account the colours and patterns of the fabrics. The designer should become adept at using colour in presentation drawings to suggest the effects of pattern and texture. The colours chosen for a design should always be accurately represented in presentation drawings.

Layout and presentation effects
Presentation drawings are used on many different occasions: when showing designs to clients, entering competitions and setting up displays, as well as for portfolio work for interviews and assessments.

Many different techniques may be used for the presentation of work. The layout and mounting need to be especially carefully considered. Photographs, sketches and decorative effects can be introduced, often as a backdrop to complement the design drawing. The photocopier can also be a valuable tool. However, you should take care never to let the presentation of your work overpower the design drawing itself. Examples of presentation drawings are given throughout the book.

Fashion illustration

The fashion illustrator works in a specialized area of advertising and marketing, producing drawings for promotional magazines and newspapers as well as publicity material for catalogues and stores. Fashion drawings are also used for window displays and exhibition stands. A further area of work is in the production of fashion prediction drawings and illustrations are also often used in packaging designs.

Fashion illustrators are often trained as such or as graphic designers. However, many illustrators start fashion drawing whilst studying on fashion design courses. Styles of drawing vary considerably. Glossy magazines and stores with a high fashion image tend to use elegant and freestyle kinds of drawing. Drawing styles are constantly changing to reflect the influences and mood of fashion at any particular time.

Some fashion designs date very swiftly. The drawings in this book have been produced over a period of a year, and while some designs are classic, others reflect changing moods and styles.

Drawing the figure

Figure proportions

The height of the average figure varies from between seven-and-a-half to eight times the height of the head. In a fashion sketch, proportions are usually eight to eight-and-a-half with the length of the leg exaggerated. Try not to overexaggerate when producing sketches, however, as this may distort the proportions of your design.

When sketching, first draw the figure with very light pencil lines and check that the positions of the chest, waist and hips are correct, as well as the overall proportions. It is helpful to add a faint line following the central contours of the body. This vertical balance line should be drawn from the nape of the neck to the foot that is carrying the weight of the body to indicate that the head and the neck are aligned with the supporting foot. This will serve as a guide when designing and positioning relative details.

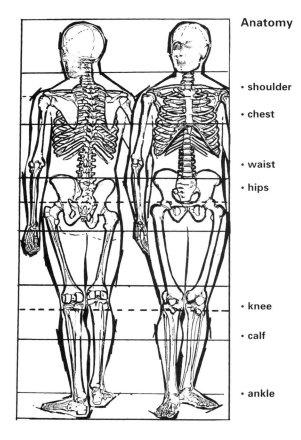

Anatomy

- shoulder
- chest
- waist
- hips
- knee
- calf
- ankle

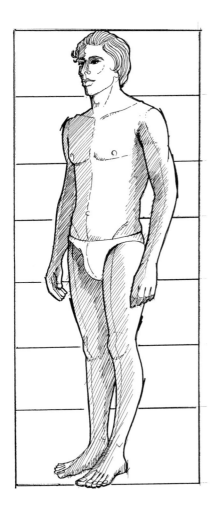
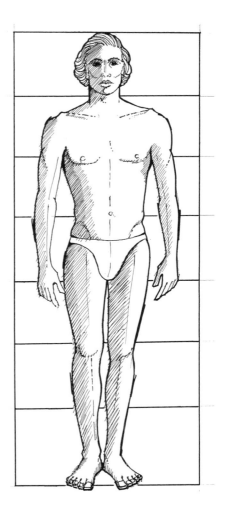

Basic figure drawing

In order to express your design ideas precisely and to present them in an attractive way, you will need to develop your skills in figure drawing. When designing, you should be able to sketch a figure from memory in a number of different poses.

Start by studying figure drawing until you can memorize the correct proportions and draw freehand figures with confidence.

I have grouped the different techniques of drawing the fashion figure under the following headings:

1   **Figure proportions.**
2   **Drawing from templates.**
3   **Drawing from the imagination**
     - stylized drawings.
4   **Drawing from photographs.**
5   **Drawing from life.**

Even if you are unable to attend life drawing and costume classes, you will find the methods illustrated in this book a valuable aid to developing your figure drawing techniques.

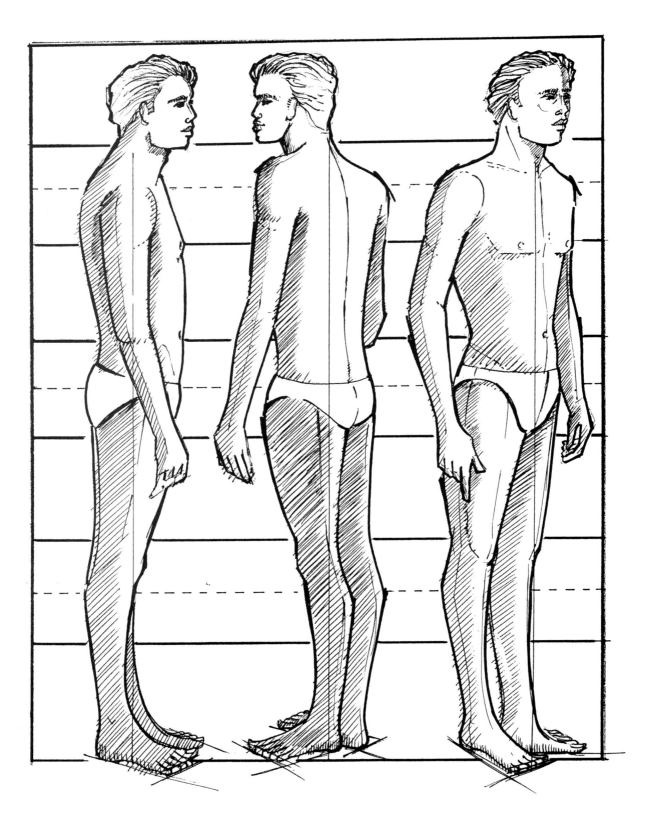

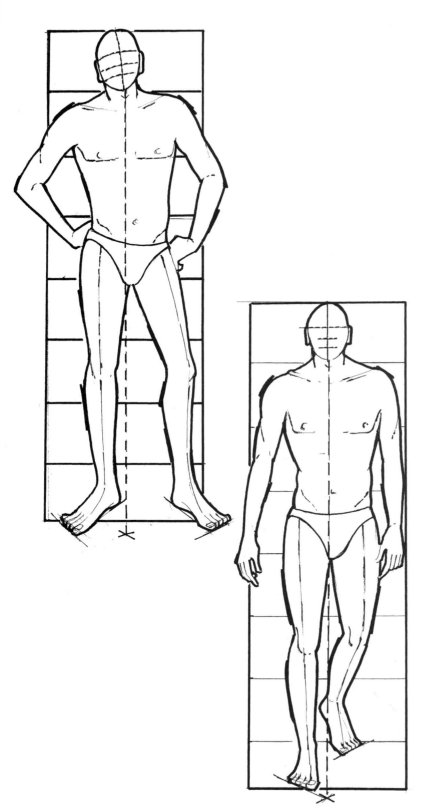

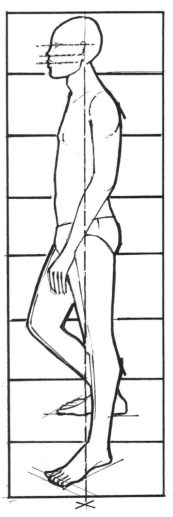

• Templates developed from life. Note how the drawings have been simplified to create a clear outline of the figure. These can be used as templates to develop your design ideas. Photocopy and enlarge templates from this book and practise designing over them, or, adapt some life drawings of your own as figure templates.

Figures in movement

It is very important to reflect the mood of the design by selecting the correct pose: for instance, one that reflects some kind of activity such as dancing or running. Different methods can be used to achieve the required effect: working from a life model, making quick sketches which may be developed afterwards, working from photographs of figures in action poses or developing a pose from the imagination using the grid. To start, try working from templates illustrated in the book or create some templates of your own.

• Sketches developed over life drawings. Note the stylized techniques, exaggerating the pose, used to emphasize the casual image. A fine Artline and a Pentel Sign pen of a different line value were used in these drawings. The pattern was developed by placing a textured surface under the layout paper and applying a soft pencil over the paper. This effect need only be suggested on the sketch, leaving areas of white to give the impression of light.

Articulated models

Another method of developing a figure in action is to visualize its different parts in terms of a cube, cylinder and sphere.

The individual parts are connected by three different types of joint:

1 **The ball and socket joint which appears at the shoulders, hips, wrists and ankles.**
2 **The hinge joint, found at the knees and elbows.**
3 **The flexible column, a term used to describe the spine and the neck.**

Each of these joints varies considerably in the type of motion it allows. You can study the possibilities and limitations of motion in the human body best by observing how your own body moves. Practise by making quick sketches based on this method. The figures shown are based on the proportions of 8 heads into the body.

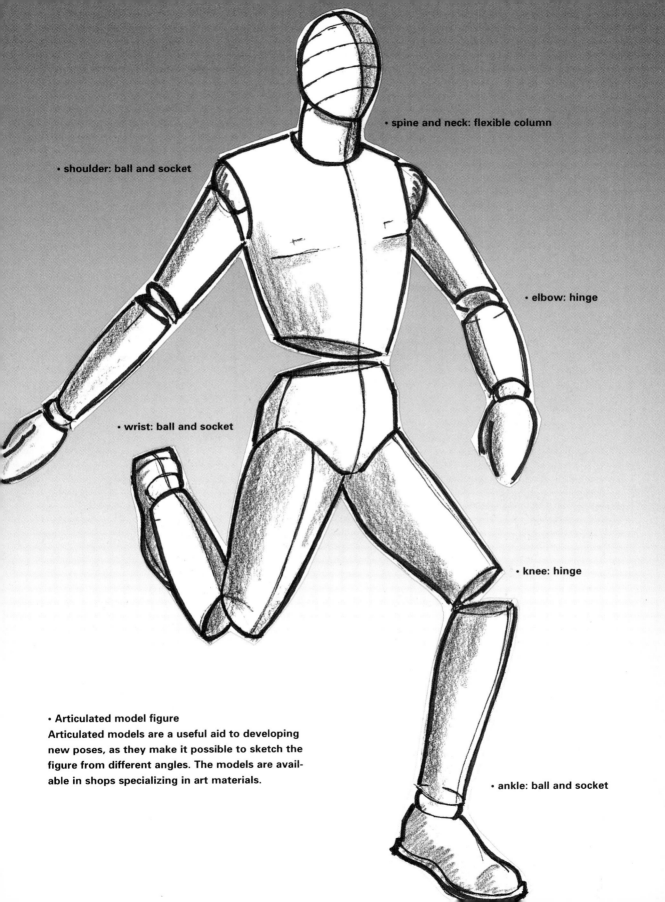

• spine and neck: flexible column

• shoulder: ball and socket

• elbow: hinge

• wrist: ball and socket

• knee: hinge

• Articulated model figure
Articulated models are a useful aid to developing
new poses, as they make it possible to sketch the
figure from different angles. The models are available in shops specializing in art materials.

• ankle: ball and socket

1   The initial figure has been developed from imagination, working on the principle of a cube, cylinder and sphere.

2   The design is sketched over the figure with the aid of layout paper.

3   The final stage of the stylized fashion sketch uses pens of different thicknesses and adds texture. Note the exaggeration of the boot and the use of folds to give the figure movement.

• Figure in running position to illustrate a sports garment. The drawing uses pen combined with a soft 4B pencil for shading. It has been cut out, allowing a white margin round the figure, and offset against an airbrushed background.

Drawing from templates

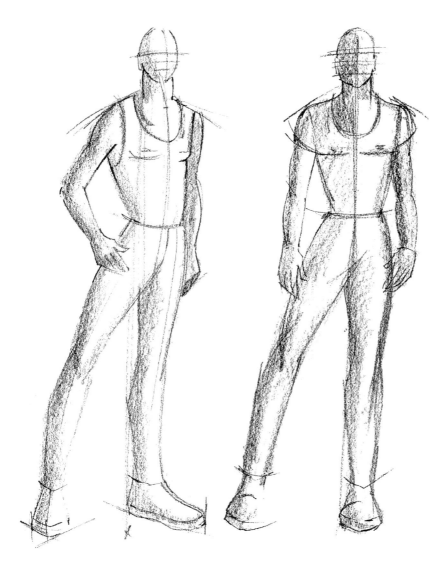

Working over templates is a quick and effective way of producing design drawings. For practice in designing over templates, either trace the figure poses in this section or, preferably, construct your own, working from the grid.

Creating and using templates

1   Sketch the figure in a free style.
2   Place layout paper over the sketch. The sketch should be clearly visible through the semi-transparent paper.
3   Develop the design template, remembering to relate to the overall proportions of the figure. The balance line falls from the nape of the neck to the feet, taking the weight of the body.

• Opposite: These templates were developed from rough sketches. The poses were drawn freely with a soft 4B pencil, observing the basic figure proportions, and were then developed by placing a transparent paper over the sketch and creating a clear line drawing suitable for designing over.

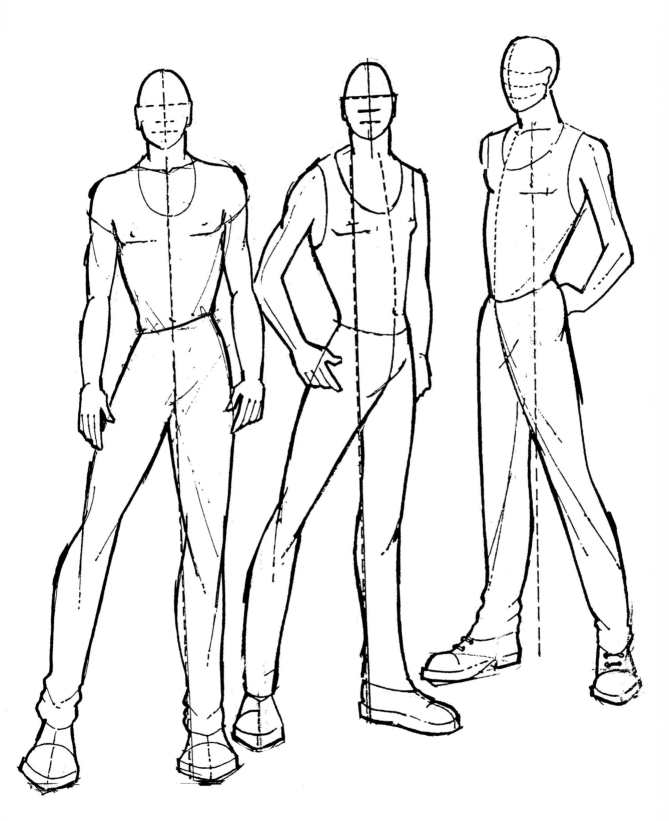

• Using a template as an aid for developing designs allows the designer to express ideas with more speed. However, some students may find it easier to sketch freely.

• Development of design ideas working over a figure template.
The resulting series of drawings may be used as a design
sheet. Note the careful attention to the placement of details
such as pockets, lapels and buttons.

• This figure pose was developed from a photograph. The design sketches were produced over the template using a free style of drawing and a Pentel pen. Texture is added by placing fabric under the paper and applying a soft coloured pencil over the surface. Note the attention given to the design details and the movement of the folds suggested by the simple use of line. Keep the figure basic to start with, merely indicating the face, hair, hands and feet.

• Each student of design develops a way of expressing ideas on paper. The design sketch may be free in style or more controlled. However, it is important when showing a collection of sketches to a client, lecturer or examiner that the drawings convey your ideas clearly.

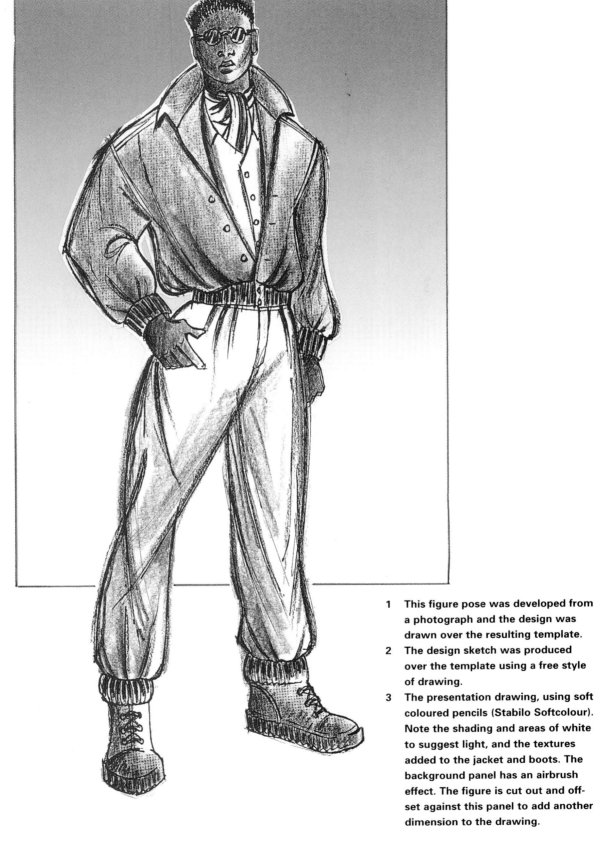

1 This figure pose was developed from a photograph and the design was drawn over the resulting template.

2 The design sketch was produced over the template using a free style of drawing.

3 The presentation drawing, using soft coloured pencils (Stabilo Softcolour). Note the shading and areas of white to suggest light, and the textures added to the jacket and boots. The background panel has an airbrush effect. The figure is cut out and off-set against this panel to add another dimension to the drawing.

Drawing from the imagination

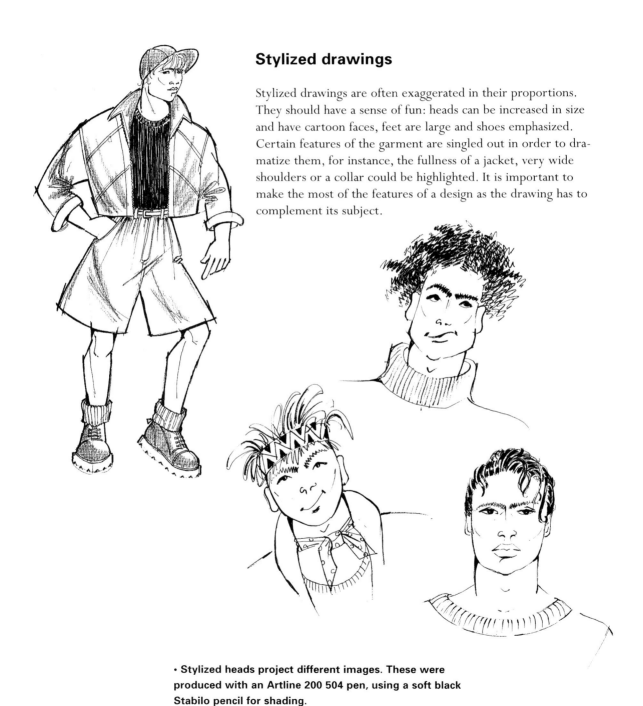

Stylized drawings

Stylized drawings are often exaggerated in their proportions. They should have a sense of fun: heads can be increased in size and have cartoon faces, feet are large and shoes emphasized. Certain features of the garment are singled out in order to dramatize them, for instance, the fullness of a jacket, very wide shoulders or a collar could be highlighted. It is important to make the most of the features of a design as the drawing has to complement its subject.

• Stylized heads project different images. These were produced with an Artline 200 504 pen, using a soft black Stabilo pencil for shading.

• **Stylized illustration: a line drawing using two pens of different thicknesses combined with a watercolour wash, produced on a smooth Bristol board.**

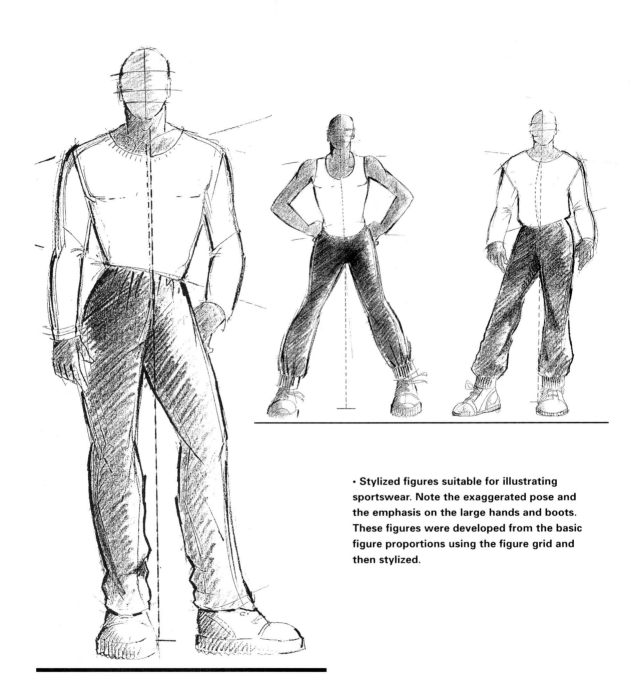

• Stylized figures suitable for illustrating sportswear. Note the exaggerated pose and the emphasis on the large hands and boots. These figures were developed from the basic figure proportions using the figure grid and then stylized.

• Stylized illustration, developed from the pose on the opposite page, using a fine pointed pen (Edding 1800) and watercolour wash for tone effects.

• A Schwan Stabilo pen
was used for the outlines
of this drawing, with a
soft pencil for the shading.

Opposite
• Presentation of a stylized sketch illustrating a ski jacket. Note the use of a photographic image in the background to offset the figure, suggesting the environment in which the garment would be worn. The sketch has been produced with a selection of Pantone marker pens of different thicknesses, with a soft black pencil indicating folds and texture and the quilting of the hood.

Drawing from photographs

Select poses from magazines and catalogues which suit the mood of your design. The figure can be static or in motion according to your needs. Although it is tempting to choose photographs which are complex and therefore look more interesting, these may not work well as drawings.

Work from straightforward poses to start with, choosing garments that clearly reveal the outline of the figure. Analyse the pose to find the position of the balance line from the neck to the load-bearing foot, and notice how the movement of the shoulders relates to the waist and hips. The centre front line is always a good guide. Keep the details simple; it is enough merely to suggest the outlines of the hands and face.

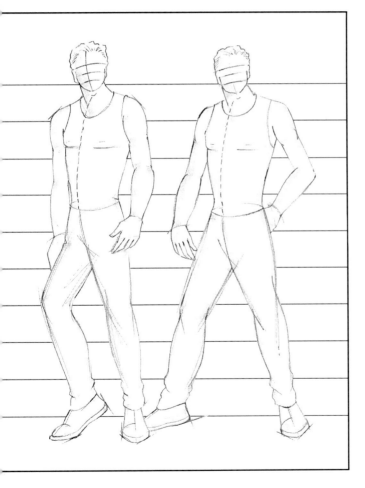

• Try sketching quick poses from a photograph.

1   Start with a pale grey marker pen (eg Pantone Grey 1M) to indicate the pose, and work into the tone with a soft pencil.

2   This kind of sketch could be developed into a template for designing over.

• Develop a number of different positions from one pose simply by changing the position of the arms and legs. Always remember to check the centre front line of the body and the position of the leg taking the weight of the body, noting how this affects the position of the hips and shoulders.

• The pose from this photograph could be used to illustrate a selection of designs, with variations achieved by changing the position of the arms, legs or head.

Photographs can be useful sources when developing new poses for your design illustrations. They are also a good reference guide for observing the details of a garment: the way in which folds appear on a sleeve or jacket; the look of collars, sleeves and trousers at different angles; pockets, belts and scarves; the folds and gathers of certain fabrics and the way in which materials fall.

Sketching from photographs will help considerably when you require new poses and a model is not available. These sketches were produced using a pale grey pantone marker pen to suggest the pose and then were developed over the tone with a soft 3B pencil. The finer details were added using an HB pencil.

When working from photographs of a garment on a model, make careful observation drawings of the details. Experiment with different pencils, crayons and paints to achieve the effect of tweeds, soft folds, knitted yarns and patterns. The texture of the paper is an important consideration, ie a textured surface for tweeds and a smooth surface for soft woollen fabrics and silk.

• Select photographs from a magazine or a catalogue to work from. Observe details carefully and note the behaviour of a collar when turned up, the fold of the sleeve and the balance of pockets, yokes and fastenings when the figure is in a three-quarters or side position. Suggest patterns and textures and study the folds and gathers. It is good practice to draw the actual garments, making careful observation drawings of specific areas: pockets, the collar, a cuff, a yoke interest.

• Select fabrics to practise suggesting patterns, checks and textures. Observe the proportions of a design or weave, remembering to take the pattern down to scale. Observe how the fabric changes when arranged in folds or draped. The pattern need only be suggested on a design sketch.

Drawing from life

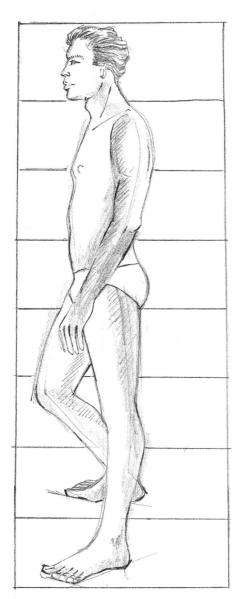

Practise creating new poses by working from the life model. Experiment by using different media and grades of paper, and try drawing varying sizes with both very free and more controlled techniques. Most fashion design courses have time allotted to life and costume drawing. The poses will vary from the very short, a few minutes, just giving you time to sketch a general outline, to more concentrated periods of 20 minutes or more. It is important to establish the pose and composition before working on the detail. Create new poses for fashion illustration by developing drawings produced in life class. Select the pose to complement the design and exaggerate features appropriate to the fashion sketch.

• A simple line drawing developed from a life pose using a 2B pencil. A 3B pencil combined with a grey marker pen is used for the shading.

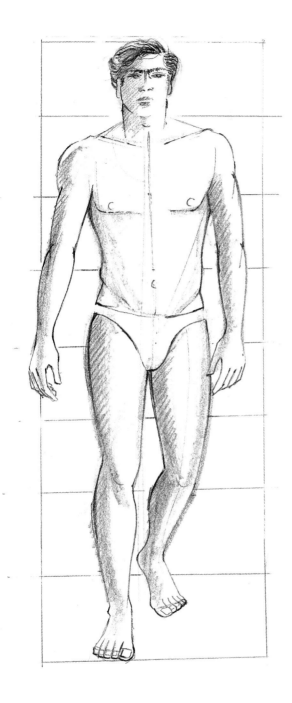

• A pencil sketch with added shading on the jumper.
The patterned effect is achieved by placing a textured
paper under the drawing and applying soft pencil over
the surface.

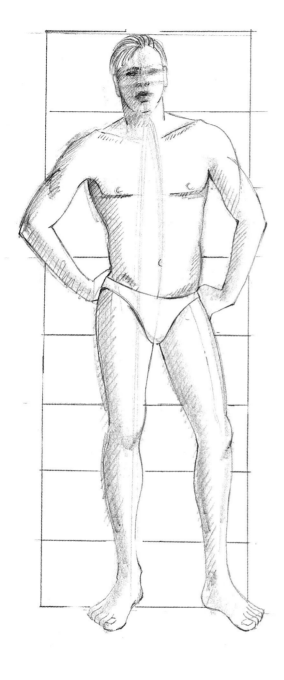

• The poses have been selected to complement the designs which use Pantone marker pens with a soft Stabilo pencil for the shading.

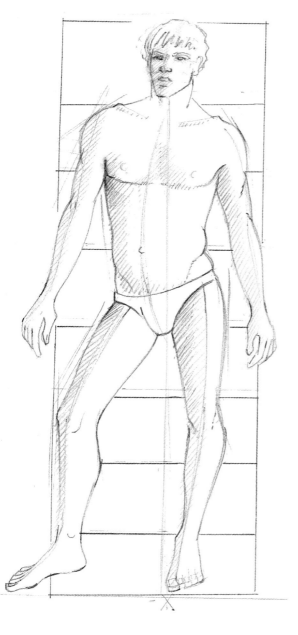

• When drawing from a model, start by observing the general pose and sketch in a few lines, noting the balance of the figure.

• Note the use of folds and shading to give the figure movement. Details of yoke, cuffs and gathers have been added with a fine line.

Heads and faces

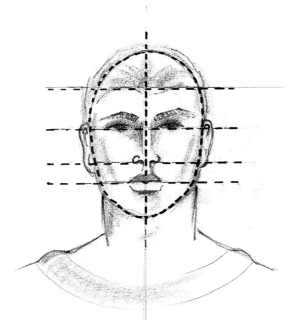

In fashion illustration, the face can merely be suggested using a few lines or worked up in greater detail. The style may be very stylized or realistic, depending on the image you wish to present through your drawing. The representation of the face and the hairstyle plays a major role in projecting the fashion image.

Observe new trends and collect photographs from fashion magazines and other media and note the many variations in styles. Keep a sketchbook of current looks, collect cuttings and note the different styles when attending fashion shows.

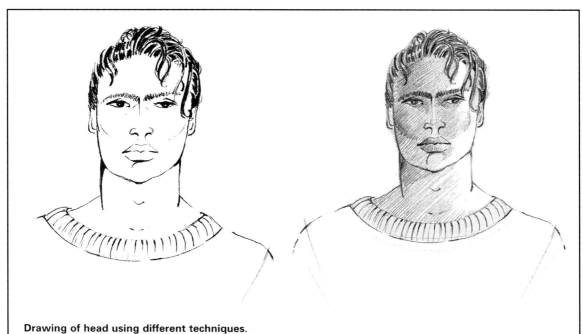

Drawing of head using different techniques.
1. Line drawing with a fine line pen.

2. Pencil drawing with shading using 2B and HB pencils.

Drawing the head

1 Halve an oval shape both vertically and horizontally.
2 The two lower parts are again divided horizontally, providing four segments.
3 The eyes are located on the centre line. The eyebrows are a quarter of the distance up from the eyes.
   The mouth is one third the distance below the nose to the chin.
4 The hairline is approximately the top quarter of the head.
5 In profile, the oval is tilted and the ear is placed behind the centre line as illustrated.
6 A line in front of the ear establishes the position of the jaw.
7 The head is illustrated with shading.

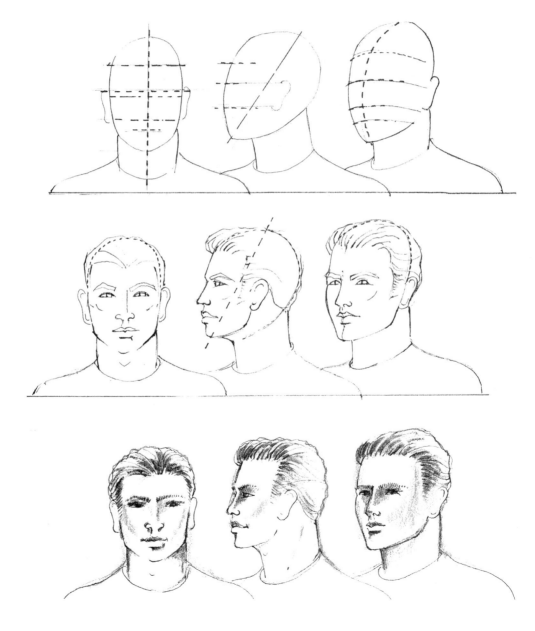

This is a simple method of drawing the head.
Note the position of the features and the guideline indicating the balance and proportions.

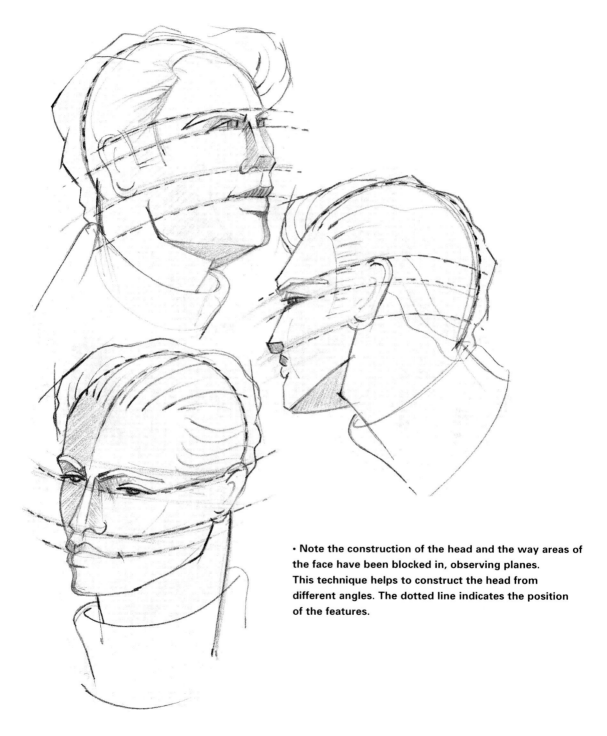

• Note the construction of the head and the way areas of the face have been blocked in, observing planes. This technique helps to construct the head from different angles. The dotted line indicates the position of the features.

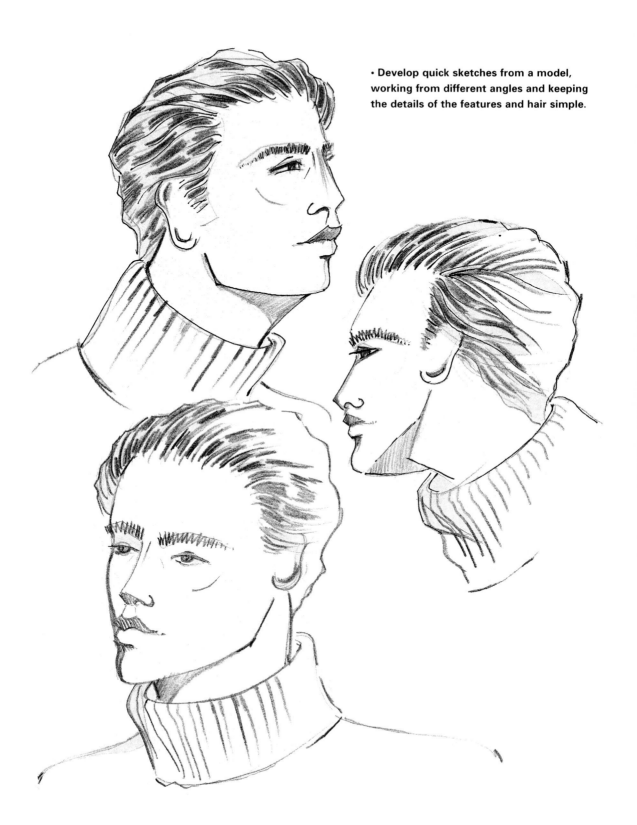

• Develop quick sketches from a model, working from different angles and keeping the details of the features and hair simple.

• Three stages in drawing the head. The final drawing was produced with a grey Pantone pen 1M for the tone and a soft black Stabilo pencil for the shading, leaving areas of white to give the effect of light.

• Stylized sketch developed with a Pantone
black marker pen and a soft black pencil.

1 Use a photograph to develop the pose of the head.

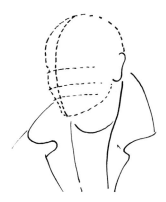

2 Analyse the features and add the balance line showing the head's position.

3 The finished pencil sketch, drawn with a soft 3D pencil on textured paper.

Select photographs from fashion magazines and work from them to develop faces and hairstyles. Simplify the features, keeping the drawings light and not overworked. Experiment with different pencils and pens, as well as a selection of papers and textures. The face need not be a likeness to the photograph.

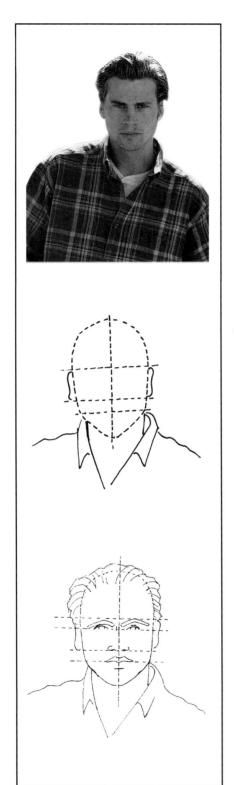

• **A simple interpretation of the face, drawn from a photograph. Note the use of textured paper.**

In fashion drawing, facial features are often only suggested with the simplest of lines. Study the features from life and draw them from different angles. Practise drawing faces from life, from photographs and from the imagination. Note the variety in facial shapes and features.

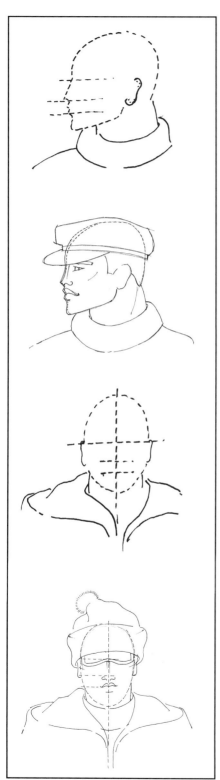

When illustrating design ideas, remember the total look projected depends on accessories as well as on the design of the garment.

Practise sketching different hat shapes, working from photographs or from a model. Note the way the hat is worn, make sketches from different angles and study the different textures and the trimmings that can be used.

Make a study of trends. Always keep a sketchbook handy and make sketches and notes of new styles for future reference.

• Note the construction of the head and the way the hat fits around the head. Keep sketches light and simple in line, merely suggesting the head and features.

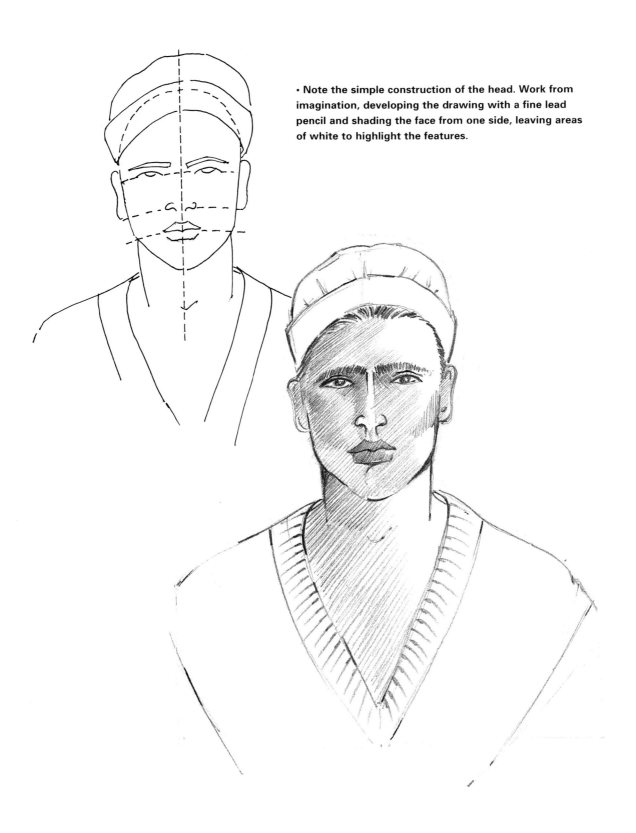

• Note the simple construction of the head. Work from imagination, developing the drawing with a fine lead pencil and shading the face from one side, leaving areas of white to highlight the features.

• A selection of caps produced with a black soft pencil. Note the shading to add dimension to the sketch.

• Hats are an important part of a fashion image.
Make notes of new styles as seen on the cat-
walk or in magazines and shop window displays. These sketches have been produced
working from a model, using a Stabilo
Softcolour pencil on a cartridge textured paper.

Hands

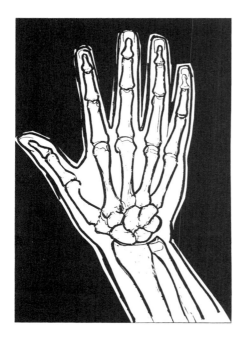

When design drawing, it is not necessary to draw the hands in great detail; often a few simple lines will be sufficient. If you find drawing the hand difficult, place it at the side of the figure or in a pocket, using only a few lines.

Make quick sketches, expressing and developing ideas from the imagination. It can be helpful to practise sketching the hands of a model from different angles, or even to draw your own.

• **Study your own hands, as well as photographs. Make anatomical sketches and devise simple ways of suggesting the hand for when producing quick design sketches. The block forms will help considerably when constructing a hand and working up the proportions.**

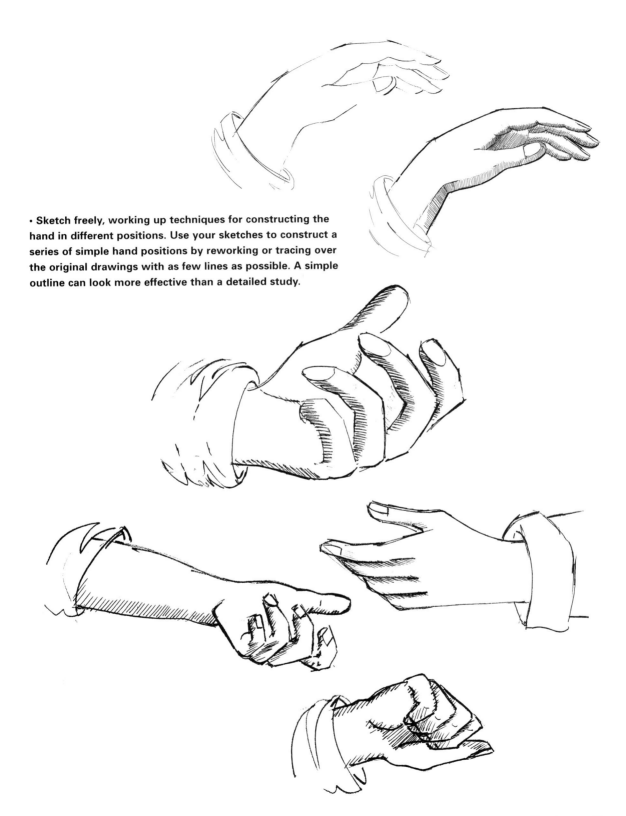

• Sketch freely, working up techniques for constructing the hand in different positions. Use your sketches to construct a series of simple hand positions by reworking or tracing over the original drawings with as few lines as possible. A simple outline can look more effective than a detailed study.

Shoes

Observation drawings

To develop confidence in drawing shoes, make careful observation drawings, placing the shoes at different angles and observing their shape and general structure, as well as the sole, heel and the upper, the fastenings, textures and any other decorative effects. Make a study of new styles that will complement a fashion image. Keep notes in your sketchbook, including details of shapes, stitching and new effects. It is important to keep abreast of current trends by studying displays in shop windows and photographs in fashion magazines.

• As an exercise, sketch different styles of shoe from various angles, experimenting with a range of techniques to achieve a variety of effects.

This sketch was developed in two stages.

1   The basic shape was sketched, paying attention to the centre front line for balance.

2   The sketch was completed with details of stitching and textures, taking into account the proportions of the shoe.

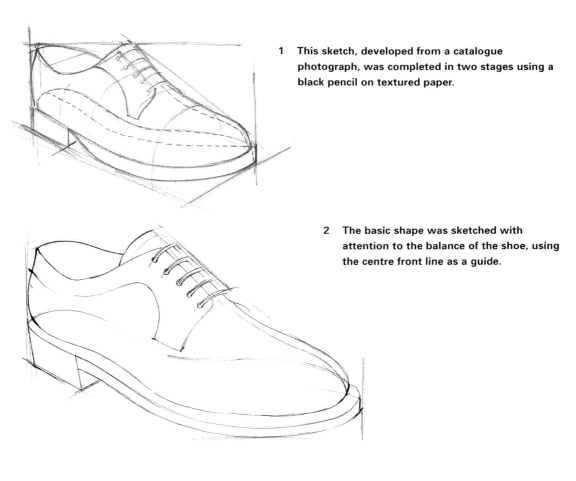

1 This sketch, developed from a catalogue photograph, was completed in two stages using a black pencil on textured paper.

2 The basic shape was sketched with attention to the balance of the shoe, using the centre front line as a guide.

3 The shading and the details were developed. Note the areas of white left to give contrast to the shading.

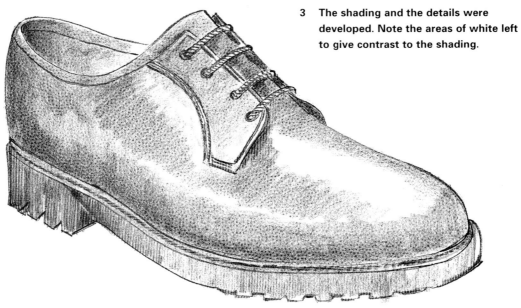

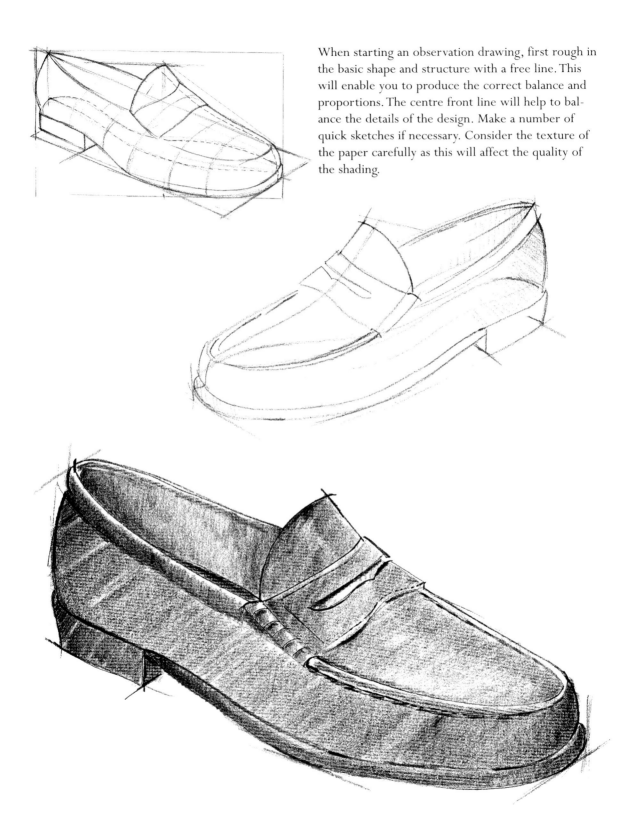

When starting an observation drawing, first rough in the basic shape and structure with a free line. This will enable you to produce the correct balance and proportions. The centre front line will help to balance the details of the design. Make a number of quick sketches if necessary. Consider the texture of the paper carefully as this will affect the quality of the shading.

1   A simple line drawing with added detail. Study the proportions of the different shapes of shoe carefully, paying attention to features such as stitching, decorative effects and lacing.

2   The development of shading. Areas are left white to suggest highlights of the leather. Note the attention given to the details of the lacing and the decorative effects of the shoe. This drawing was produced on a rough textured paper using a 3B pencil, and details were added with a fine pen.

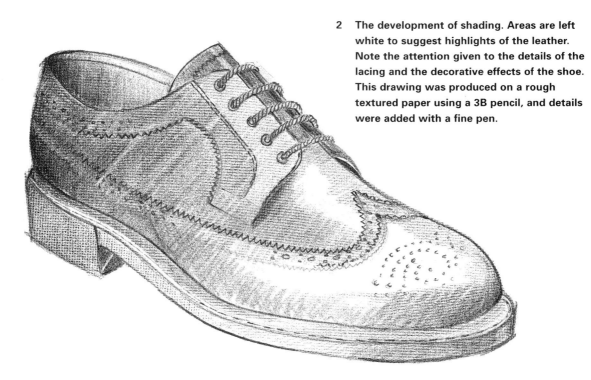

• With a more complicated shoe, study features such as proportion, stitching, lacing and thickness of the sole before starting the sketch.

1 Outline of a boot, working in a free style. One shape is related to another in order to achieve the correct effect.

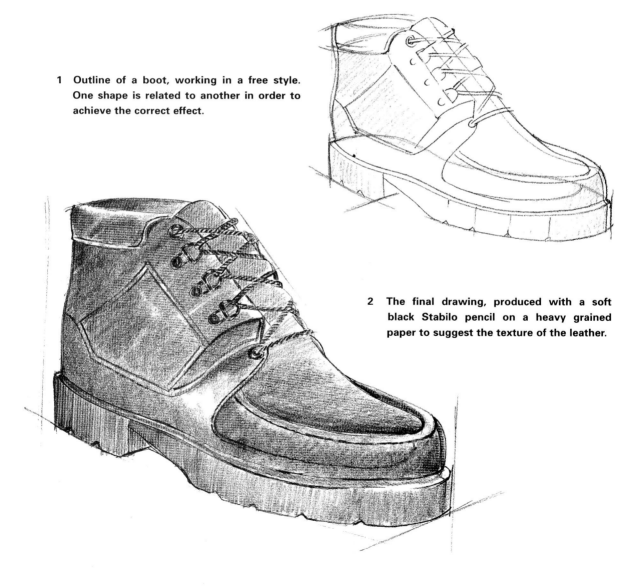

2 The final drawing, produced with a soft black Stabilo pencil on a heavy grained paper to suggest the texture of the leather.

• Stylized sketches showing textured effects. Make quick sketches when working on themed ideas, adding notes and leather samples to indicate colour and texture.

Drawing fashion details

Observation drawings

Design detail drawings are often combined with working sketches to give complete information about a particular feature such as cuffs, collars, seams, pockets and fastenings. This type of drawing must convey every detail without exaggeration.

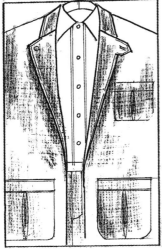

• **Patch pockets with inverted pleats**

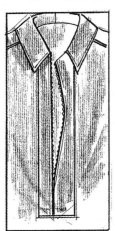

• **Front panel with zip fastening opening**

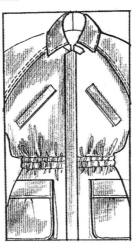

• **Raglan sleeve; welt pockets; fly front opening; elasticated waist; patch pockets with flaps**

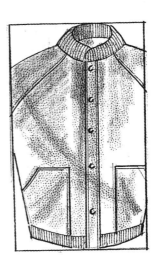

• **Raglan sleeve; ribbed stand collar; front button opening; patch pockets from side seam; ribbed waist band**

• Design detail drawings showing variations in neckline, colars
and lapels as well as a selection of pockets and fabric textures.

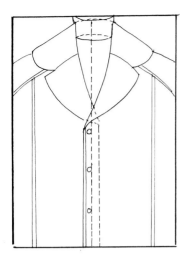

It is important to study fashion magazines and attend fashion shows in order to observe the season's trends. Make careful detail drawings together with notes of special features, fabrics and colours. Always consider the image projected by the design.

1 **Collar in contrast fabric, raglan sleeve, seam pockets with stand from front panels and single-breasted button fastening.**

2 **Single-breasted jacket with a four-button fastening, worn with a shirt with a stand collar and a high-buttoned waistcoat, and patch pockets including seam interest.**

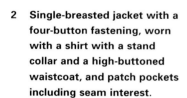

3 **Double breasted jacket with button fastening, welt pockets, collar and large lapel.**

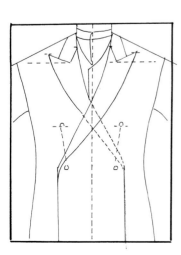

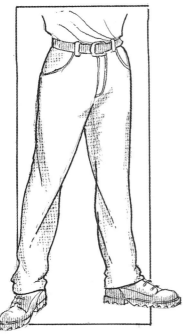

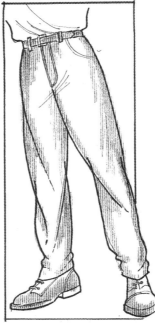

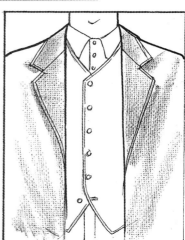

• A selection of design details, with textures added, using a Pentel Sign pen for the illustrations and a finer Artline pen for details such as seaming.

• Saddle sleeve

• Raglan
sleeve

• Sportswear overshirt in gortex fabric; deep set-in
sleeve with zipped fastening at wrist; panel at neck
with front zip fastening; large collar with stand, large
patch pockets with side openings.

• Dropped shoulder line

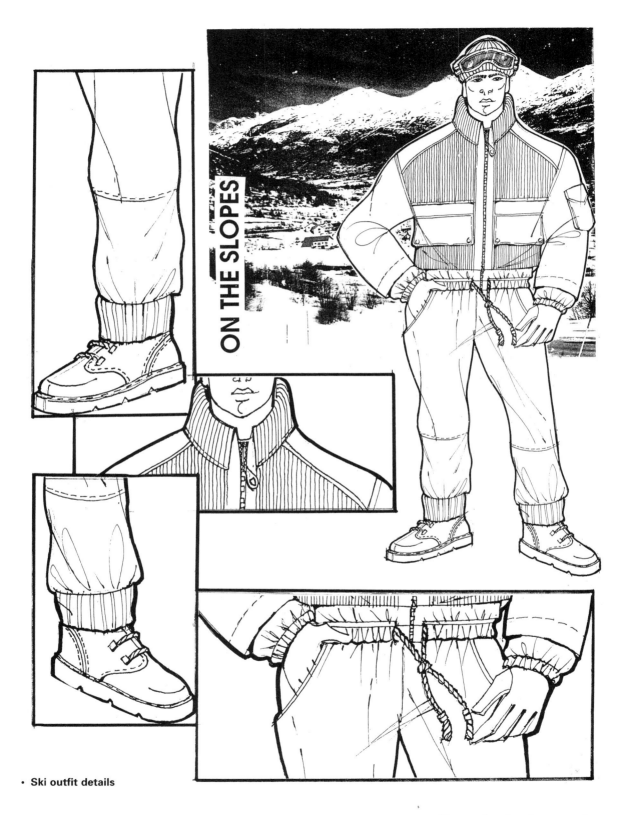

ON THE SLOPES

• **Ski outfit details**

Production drawings

A production drawing is sometimes known as a working drawing or a flat. When a garment design has been approved and a sample is requested, the production team will need a specification sheet and production drawing. This drawing has to be diagrammatic in order to show details of the cut, seam and dart placement, and the proposed style features. Detailed production drawings will also be needed for the final design specification which will go to the factory where the garments are to be made.

It is important to study how garments are put together so that the structure of your designs can be represented in the production drawing clearly and with accuracy.

This style of drawing is also used professionally when drawing for fashion prediction books and forecasting fashion trends.

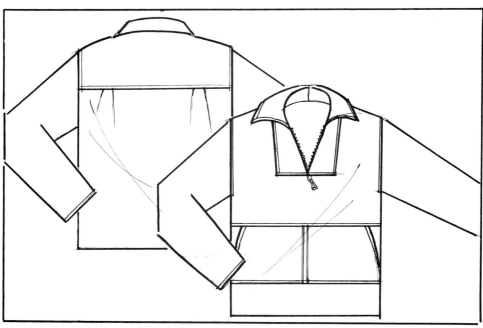

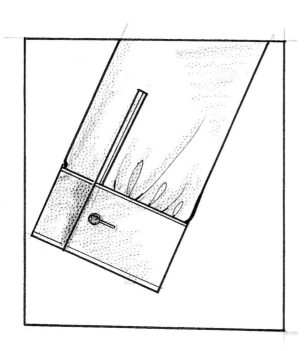

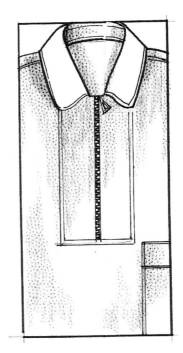

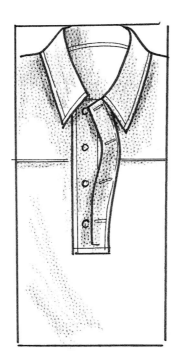

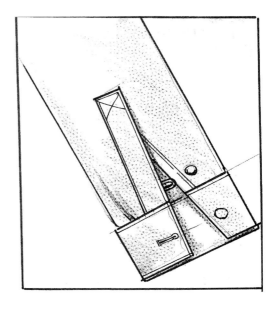

• Observation drawings of details from garments, shown in a clear and diagrammatical style.

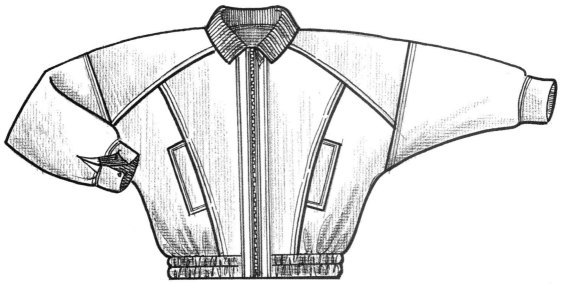

• Casual blouson jacket in fine cord fabric, deep set-in sleeves;
shoulder yokes; panel feature emphasized with seams, seam
pockets in panels; centre front zip opening with contrast
corded collar and cuff lining; elasticated waist; yoke with
panel interest and gathers at the back of the waist.

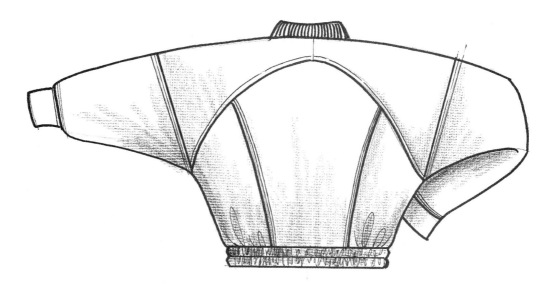

• Shorts with three rows of elastication at waist, with a button fastening, fly front and cuffs on the trousers.

• Sports shirt; stand collar; four-button fastening; short sleeves; yoke with large patch pockets and seam interest; back yoke with full gathers.

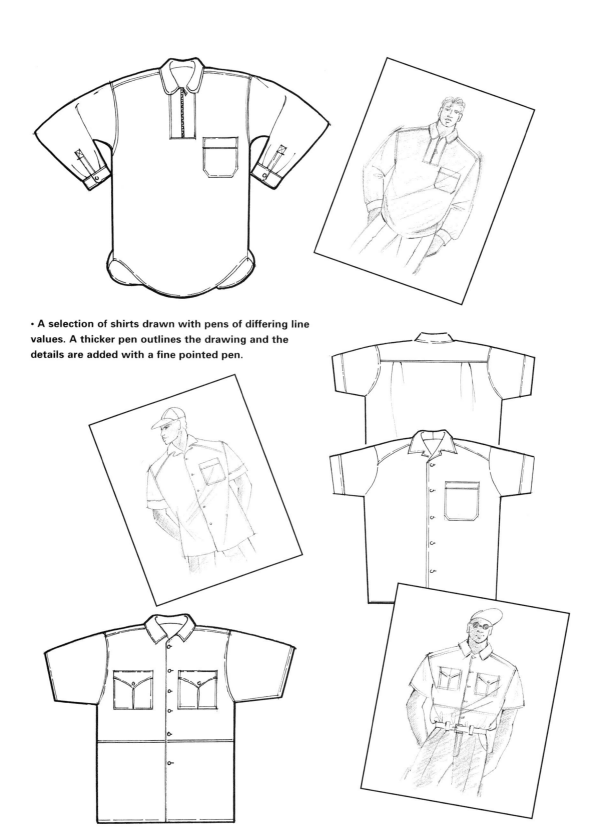

• A selection of shirts drawn with pens of differing line values. A thicker pen outlines the drawing and the details are added with a fine pointed pen.

• **Presentation board mounted on card, with fashion sketch and emphasis on the working drawing.**

Patterns and textures

Textured and pattern effects can be developed with the aid of a selection of materials such as canvas, fabric, embossed paper and net. Placing a lightweight paper, such as layout paper, over the textured material and rubbing over the surface with a soft pencil creates a textured impression.

It is useful to collect a folder of interesting textures for use when illustrating. Experiment with different pencils. Attaching the textured pieces to thick card will give you a firmer surface on which to work.

It is not always necessary to reproduce every detail of the pattern on your sketch: perhaps simply suggest it on one side of the figure. Showing the pattern on the cross is a useful way of indicating the cut of the material.

As an exercise, produce a number of sketches or photocopy one several times. Experiment with different effects using, for instance, watercolour, pastels or crayons.

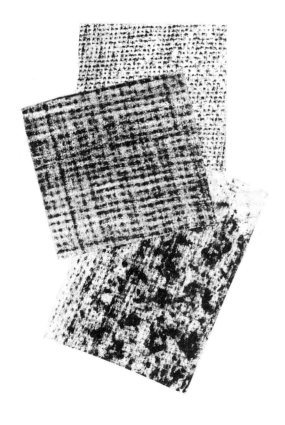

• **Soft pencils**

• Watercolour

• Crayon and pastels

Patterns and textures

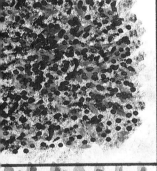

Left: Experiment with patterns and textures, making notes in your sketchbook. Work with a variety of different materials, such as wax crayons, marker pens, paints, watercolours and gouache, and practise suggesting tweeds, checks, fur and leather.

Below: This sketch incorporates a selection of textures, produced by placing materials such as canvas, embossed paper and hessian under the paper and applying pencil over the surface.

Techniques and presentation

Collage

A collage is a composition of materials applied to a background. It is a very effective way of demonstrating patterns and flat colour with cut-out shapes. This technique has many possibilities for presentation work as it can vary from a very free and abstract approach to a controlled and neat effect.

- Sketch drawn from a model.
1 The sketch is developed into a line drawing by working over it with the aid of a light box. The fabric pattern is reduced to scale on the photocopier, and sections of the shirt traced over the line drawing using the light box. Corresponding sections of pattern copy are cut out and applied to the drawing.
2 Presentation design board (opposite): Areas of white are left to indicate folds, collar and other style details. The figure is placed against a background which suggests the environment in which the garment would be worn and the drawing is completed with marker pens.

1   Sketch drawn from a model.
2   Pattern pieces are applied to the figure.
3   Opposite: The final presentation drawing, combined with a
    working drawing. The figure has been cut out and placed
    against an appropriate background.

Experiment with collage to create different effects, working both in a controlled way and then in a much freer style. Materials from paper to fabric can be used; tissue paper is also very effective.

• **Two stages of a presentation drawing using collage techniques.**

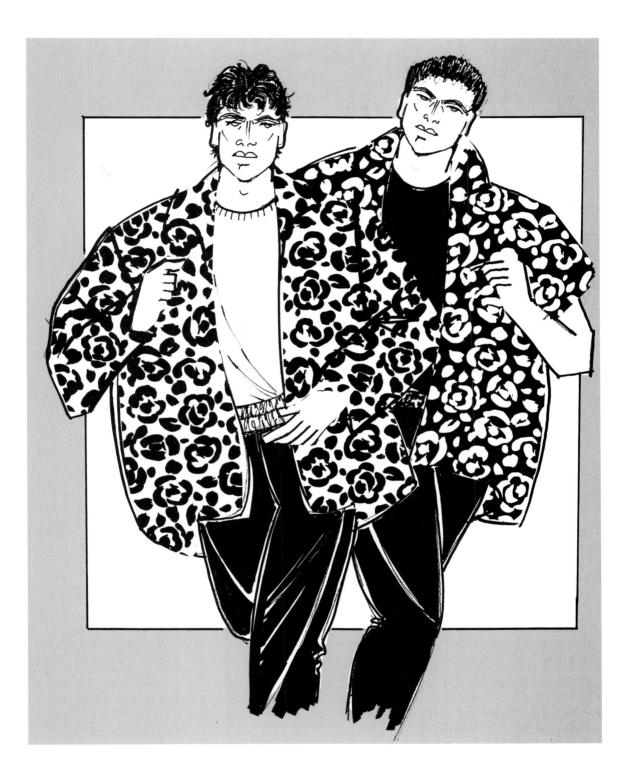

• Presentation board: The figures have been cut out and mounted against a panel, then placed on to a sheet of contrasting coloured card. Fabric has been applied to these figures to illustrate the shirts. Pentel pens were used on the trousers and T-shirts, and the details were drawn in with a fine Artline pen.

Collage 85

Materials

It is important to experiment with different materials, trying out effects and exploring possibilities. There are a great many types available, and some of the more popular are demonstrated in this section.

The cost and quality of art materials varies. Select what you require very carefully. It is not always necessary to buy large quantities. Items such as marker pens, pens, inks and pastels may be purchased individually or in small packs.

It is vital to take care of materials. Before starting work, make sure that pencils are sharp, pens clean, and brushes and mixing palettes washed and dried ready for use. Marker pen caps must always be replaced or else the pens will dry out quickly. Keep all your materials in a box and in good order so that they are easily available. Always have a selection of layout, cartridge and watercolour paper in your folder ready for use.

Work should be kept clean and flat. Always date it, and arrange it according to project themes. Have a folder of work ready to present at any time, so that you are prepared for interviews and assessments. You should always approach your work in a professional way. In design studios, you will often have a working area allocated to you, with a drawing desk and a pinboard on which to display research material.

Pens

When selecting a pen, experiment with it first to see if it produces the line required. The paper or card you use also has to be considered as its surface will affect the line value of the pen.

• Line drawing produced using two pens of differing line values.

The pens used for line drawing may be divided into five groups:
1   **Technical pens**
2   **Plastic-tip pens**
3   **Fibre-tip pens**
4   **Roller pens**
5   **Ball-point pens**

Coloured pencils

There is a wide range of colour pencils, graded from soft to hard. Some are water-solvent and may be combined with water for application with a brush in order to give a watercolour effect.

Always experiment with pencils before applying them to the drawing. The more pressure applied, the more intense the colour will be. Select a rough or smooth surface paper, depending on the effect you require, remembering to use an absorbent paper when applying water.

• **Illustration using Schwan Stabilo soft colour pencils. These can be used with solvent based markers or turpentine. Colours can be blended by applying layers on top of each other.**

Plastic-tipped pens

These produce very fine, accurate lines.

Fibre-tipped pens

The nibs of these pens are made from vinyl or nylon, and vary from firm to supple. They are made in a selection of sizes for different line values.

Roller pens

These have a very smooth action that produce an even flow of ink. A range of colours and widths are available.

Ball-point pens

The point of these pens is made from a steel ball that rolls. They are available in a range of colours and widths.

Technical pens

The ink pens used by designers are known as technical pens. They produce a clear line, the nib of the pen being in the shape of a tube. The ink is fed down the tube, the size of which produces the width of the line. Technical pens are extremely accurate for very fine detailed work.

Inks

Pen and ink creates immediate visual effects in both line and tone. The latter may take the form of lines, dots, hatching or cross-hatching. Ink drawings combined with washes of coloured inks are most effective. Inks can be used on their own, mixed together or diluted with water.

• Line work can often use pens with different line values within the same drawing. This illustration is shaded with a soft black Stabilo pencil. Hessian was placed under the paper and pencil applied over the surface to achieve the effect of a checked shirt and tweed trousers. Note the areas of white left on the sketch.

Watercolour

Watercolour may be bought as
solid tablets or as paste in tubes to
be thinned with water before use.
Paintboxes of different sizes are
widely available. Paintbrushes vary
in quality from sable to nylon. The
paper surface is important. Unless
you are using good quality paper,
it should be stretched. If this is
not done, the paper will react to
the water by cockling, and your
work will be distorted.

**• Drawing produced with a Pentel Sign
pen, with watercolour washes added.
The illustration has been cut out and
mounted against an airbrush background for presentation.**

Pastels

Although no brushes are used, working with pastels is more akin to painting than drawing, with the advantage that there is no liquid and hence no drying time to consider. The range of tints in each colour is considerable. A variety of tones can be achieved by treating the tinted paper as a mid-tone, and a coloured paper can be used as a key for the rest of the colour scheme. The effects vary depending on which part of the pastel stick is used.

Gouache

Gouache is similar to watercolour, but is mixed with white pigment which makes it opaque. When dry, gouache forms a positive film of colour. It is associated with hard divisions of solid colour. A free style of painting may also be achieved where the brush strokes are visible. Watercolour paper or boards are most suitable for gouache; cartridge and layout papers are not suitable.

• Black and white drawing, sketched with an Artline 204 pen on Bristol board white card. This smooth card is suitable for work in ink, marker pens and watercolour. Tone values are suggested with grey gouache.

• Note the effect of the black sheepskin jacket. The wax crayon was applied to a textured paper, allowing areas of white for details. Cord trousers are suggested by scratching into the surface of the wax.

Wax and water-solvent crayons

Wax crayons are available in different thicknesses. A solid, bright colour can be achieved, and the harder the pressure, the deeper the tone. Some crayons are wax-based, which enables you to scratch into them for surface and texture effects. Others are water-based and may be used combined with water.

Wax-resistant effects

A wax crayon or candle may be used as a resistant to watercolour and inks. Firstly, mark the paper with the candle or crayon. The marked area will then repel the water-based solutions. Therefore, when a wash is added, the area will remain free of colour. A rubber solution produces a similar effect.

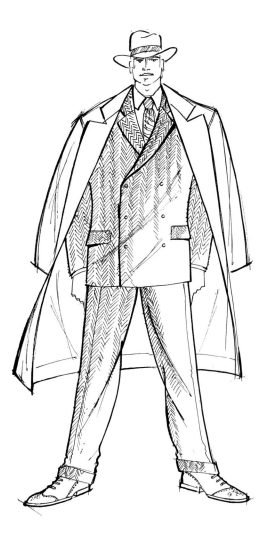

• **Line drawing using different line values. Note areas of white left on the suit to suggest light.**

Marker pens

Marker pens are available in a wide range of colours and sizes, with the many different nib types including cylinder-shaped heads, blunt bullet-like points, wedge shapes and fine points. The inks are either water-soluble or spirit-based. Markers can be used for filling in areas of colour or for making bold outlines to give a clean effect. They are extremely convenient as they dry rapidly and have great clarity of colour.

Light box

This is a box used for tracing which has a glass top and contains a light. When the work to be traced is placed under a sheet of paper resting on the glass, it is illuminated by the light below. These boxes are available in a range of sizes.

Airbrush

The airbrush provides perfect even tones, graded tones and soft lines. It will also blend colour. It is operated by a motor compressor or compressed air propellant aerosols.

Layout paper

White layout detail paper has an ideal surface for ink and pencil work. The paper is semi-transparent, which is useful when working over roughs and developing work.

Spraymount

Spraymount comes in an aerosol and allows drawings to be mounted and re-positioned. It can be used on the thinnest of tissue papers. Do not overspray your drawings and only use in a well-ventilated room.

Photocopiers

The photocopier is an invaluable tool for the fashion design illustrator. It can be used to:

1 enlarge and reduce drawings.
2 reproduce drawings on which to experiment with colour, pattern and texture techniques before working on the original.
3 produce material for background effects on presentation boards.

• **Pantone marker pens combined with soft Stabilo pencils for texture and shading.**

4 transfer drawings on to different coloured papers.

5 transfer drawings and photographs on to acetate, which is very effective for presentation work.

6 paste up drawings when working on the arrangement for design work. Cut out the figures and general artwork, and use Spraymount to fix it on to a clean white card. Photocopy in black and white or colour for a clean, professional look.

7 photocopy artwork for reference when sending your originals off for competitions etc.

8 photocopy reference work when researching and collecting material for sketchbooks and storyboards.

9 enlarge sections of design drawings such as details of collars, pockets and other style features.

10 photocopy textured and patterned materials, reducing the size to match the scale of the drawing when using collage.

11 photocopy airbrush effects for backgrounds. Use Spraymount to attach your artwork to this background.

Layout and presentation

Communication is the aim of fashion drawing. It is important that your design ideas should be clearly understood and that the information is presented in a professional and attractive way. Consider the presentation of your work before you start on the design brief.

When working on design briefs, keep a project notebook and sketchbook of research ideas, dates to which you must work and a checklist of things that need to be done. It could include:

1 research for design ideas working on a theme.
2 storyboards and moodboards reflecting your theme, including research considering the market for which you are designing, fabrics and colour. These boards are very important, especially when giving a presentation.
3 sample collections and your colour scheme.

4 initial design development sheets.
5 presentation of final design collection, giving front and back views, sample fabrics and colour.
6 working drawings and detailed drawings of final designs.
7 in some instances, toiles and made-up garments are required, and are often modelled and accessorised for your final assessment.

• When creating presentation boards, experiment with layout ideas before making a final decision. Keep abreast of fashions in graphics by studying magazines, marketing promotions and displays.

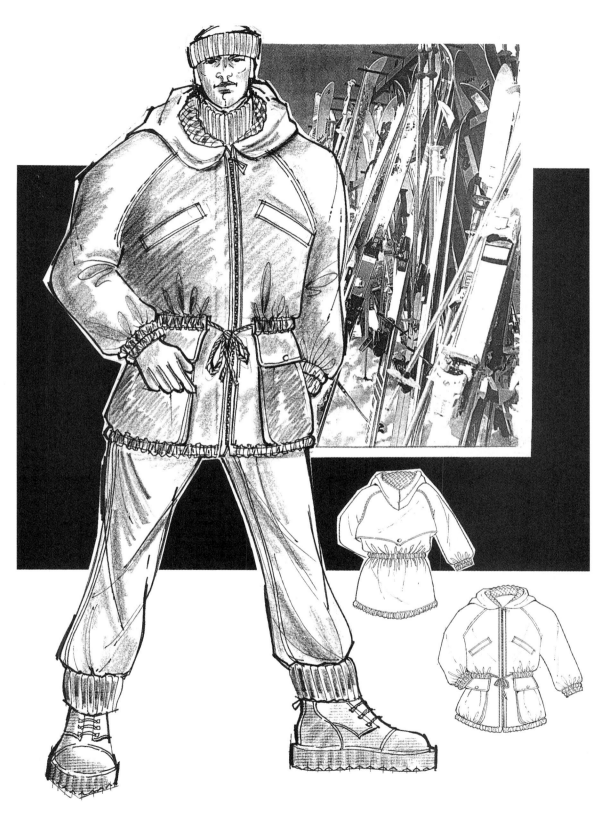

Book list

FASHION ILLUSTRATION

Barnes, Colin, *Fashion Illustration*, Macdonald, 1988

Drake, Nicholas, *Fashion Illustration Today*, Thames and Hudson, 1987

Ireland, Patrick John, *Fashion Design*, Cambridge University Press, 1987

Ireland, Patrick John, *Fashion Design Drawing and Illustration*, B.T. Batsford Ltd, 1982

Ireland, Patrick John, *Encyclopedia of Fashion Details*, B.T. Batsford Ltd, 1989

FIGURE DRAWING

Gordon, Louise, *Anatomy and Figure Drawing*, B.T. Batsford Ltd, 1988

Gordon, Louise, *Drawing the Human Head*, B.T. Batsford Ltd

Gordon, Louise, *The Figure in Action*, B.T. Batsford Ltd

Richer, Paul, *Artistic Anatomy*, Pitman

Sheppard, Joseph, *Realistic Figure Drawing*, North Light Books

GRAPHICS

Powell, Dick and Monahan, Patricia, *Advanced Marker Techniques*, Little, Brown

Shother, Jane, *The Coloured Pencil Artist's Pocket Palette*, B.T. Batsford Ltd

Smith, Ray, *The Artist's Handbook*, Dorling Kindersley

Takamura, Zeshu, *The Use of Markers in Fashion Illustrations*

REFERENCE

Illustrators Reference Manual: Hands and Faces, Bloomsbury

Illustrator's Reference Manual: Sport, Bloomsbury

FASHION HISTORY

Ames, Hardie, *The Englishman's Suit*, Quartet Books

Ewing, Elizabeth and Mackrell, Alice, *History of Twentieth Century Fashion*, B.T. Batsford Ltd, 1992

Chenoune, Farid, *A History of Men's Fashion 1760-1990s*

Druesedow, Jean L., *Men's Fashion Illustration from the Turn of the Century*

Peacock, John, *The Chronicle of Western Costume*, Thames & Hudson, 1986

Polhemus, Ted, *Street Style*, Thames & Hudson

Versace, Gianni, *Men Without Ties*, Abbeville Press

MAGAZINES

Collezioni Uomo (2 yearly)

Harpers Bazaar Uomo (6 yearly)

Harpers Bazaar Uomo Special Collections (2 yearly)

L'Uomo Vogue (11 yearly)

Vogue Hommes International (2 yearly)

Sportswear International Eur. (6 yearly)

Sportswear International (8 yearly)

Sutton, S. R. (1982). Fear-arousing communications: a critical examination of theory and research. In Eiser, J. R. (ed.) *Social psychology and behavioral medicine*. Chichester: Wiley, pp. 303–37.

Sutton, S. R. (1992). Shock tactics and the myth of the inverted U. *British Journal of Addiction*, **87**, 517–19.

Sutton, S. and Hallett, R. (1988). Smoking intervention in the work place using videotapes and nicotine chewing gum. *Preventive medicine*, **17**, 48–59.

Tolsma, D. D. (1993). Patient education objectives in Healthy People 2000: policy and research issues. *Patient Education and Counseling*, **22**, 7–14.

Tongue, B. and Stanley, I. (1991). A video-based information system for health patients. *Health Trends*, **23**, 11–12.

Vogler, R. E., Weissbach, T. A., Compton, J. V., and Martin, G. T. (1977). Integrated behaviour change techniques for problem drinkers in the community. *Journal of Consulting and Clinical Psychology*, **45**, 267–79.

Weinstein, N. D. (1983). Reducing unrealistic optimism about illness susceptibility. *Health Psychology*, **2**, 11–20.

Wilson, M. (1989). The natural history of a video programme 'Stroke: the caring for someone at home'. *Health Bulletin*, **47**, 234–7.

Zwick, R. and Attkisson, C. C. (1984). The use of reception checks in client pretherapy orientation research. *Journal of Clinical Psychology*, **40**, 446–52.

Health Education Authority, Public Health Division Research Department and Mills Hopper Associates (1990). *Pretesting of teenage smoking video: qualitative research document.* HEA.

Heilveil, I. (1983) *Video in mental health practice – an activities handbook.* London: Tavistock Publications.

Hughes, B. R., Altman, D. G., and Newton, J. A. (1993). Melanoma and skin cancer: evaluation of a health education program for secondary schools. *British Journal of Dermatology*, **128**, 412–17.

Janis, I. L. (1967). Effects of fear arousal on attitude change: recent developments in theory and research. In Berkowitz, L.(ed.) *Advances in experimental social psychology*, vol. 3. New York: Academic Press, pp. 166–224.

Janis, I. L. and Feshbach, S. (1953). Effects of fear-arousing communications. *Journal of Abnormal and Social Psychology*, **48**, 78–92.

Janz, N. K. and Becker, T. (1984). The health belief model: a decade later. *Health Education Quarterly*, **40**, 107–12.

Kahneman, D. and Tversky, A. (1979) Prospect theory: an analysis of decision under risk. *Econometrica*, **47**, 263–91.

March, J. G. (1996). Learning to be risk averse. *Psychological Review*, **103**, 309–19.

McGuire, W. J. (1964). Inducing resistance to persuasion: some contemporary approaches. In Berkowitz, L. (ed.). *Advances in experimental social psychology*, vol. 1. New York: Academic Press, pp. 191–229.

Morphy, L. A. (1984). *Feasibility study of the use of video in education and preparation for parenthood.* Research report. University of Leicester, Centre for Mass Communication Research.

Moss, R. (1983). *Video: the educational challenge.* Beckenham: Croom Helm.

Nielsen, E. and Sheppard, M. A. (1988). Television as a patient education tool: a review of its effectiveness. *Patient Education and Counseling*, **11**, 3–16.

O'Donnell, L., San Doval, A., Vornfett, R., and DeJong, W. (1994). Reducing AIDS and other STDs among inner-city Hispanics: the use of qualitative research in the development of video-based patient education. *AIDS Education and Prevention*, **6**, 104–53.

Pinnington, A. (1992). *Using video in training and education.* Maidenhead: McGraw-Hill.

Probert, C. S. J., Frisby, S., and Mayberry, J. F. (1991). Editorial: The role of educational videos in gastroenterology. *Journal of Clinical Gastroenterology*, **13**, 620–1.

Prochaska, J. O. and DiClemente, C. C. (1983). Stages and processes of self-change of smoking: toward a more integrative model of change. *Journal of Consulting and Clinical Psychology*, **51**, 390–5.

Rosenstock, I. M. (1966). Why people use health services. *Milbank Memorial Fund Quarterly*, **44**, 94–127.

Rowley, P. T., Fisher, L., and Lipkin, M. (1979). Screening and genetic counseling for Beta-Thalassemia trait in a population unselected for interest: effects on knowledge and mood. *American Journal of Human Genetics*, **31**, 718–30.

Shipley, R. H., Butt, J. H., and Horwitz, E. A. (1979). Preparation to reexperience a stressful medical examination: effect of repetitious videotape exposure and coping style. *Journal of Consulting and Clinical Psychology*, **48**, 485–92.

Susser, I. and Gonzalez, M. A. (1992). Sex, drugs and videotape: the prevention of AIDS in a New York City shelter for homeless men. *Medical Anthropology*, **14**, 307–22.